From the heart

By

S.J Warner.

Much love

S. J xxx

For C

x

Contents.

Salvation.

Hot rivers of pain fall

Tightness around the chest

A vice like feeling

Making it so hard to breathe

Heart aching

A stabbing sensation

Like someone has thrust

A knife through its centre

Soul and mind

Withering and dying

This agonising feeling

Is unbearable

Body curling into

A foetal position

Trying to become small

To hide from the torment

A tortured soul

That's hurt so much

Hoping, waiting,

Praying for salvation.

Missing you.

I miss you

It's that simple

My heart aches

Every second that

You're away

It wasn't meant

To hurt this much

And yet

It does

So very much

You see

I love you

And without you

My light has gone

My world is empty

I know

You'll return

But until that day

I shall sit here

Waiting patiently

My love

My life

My protector

The one who makes

My heart beat faster

I love you my darling

These thoughts

Are sent

From me to you

Forever your good girl.

Nightmare.

Lying here in the dark

Breathing harsh

Heartbeat fast

The monster

From my dream

Is here in the room

With me

I can smell

Its foul breath

Hear its evil chuckle

Know that it is waiting

For me to close my eyes

Before it pounces

And takes me to hell

My body is frozen

Fear overtaking me

Too scared to move

Unable to run

Cold fear gripping

My thoughts

My heart

Am I awake

Or still dreaming?

My eyes are open

But not seeing

I can feel myself

Shaking

Trapped by the terror

Screaming as I feel

Something touch my skin

Softly shaking me

Trying to pull me

From danger

It's you

You're here

Holding me tight

Against your body

As the nightmare fades

My knight in shining armour

Charging to the rescue

Slaying the beast

With your love.

Your Return.

The sun shines

As I sit waiting

Waiting for your return

My soul sings

As the fingers

On the clock

Move towards

That special time

Too long I have

Been waiting

Each day passing

So very slowly

The never ending

Tick of the clock

My emotions

All over the place

So here I sit

In the chair

By the window

Watching

Heart racing

Our house has seemed

So empty

Without you

The tick of the clock

The pounding

Of my heart

The only sounds

I hear

A smile on my face

Threatening to

Take over

And then I see it

Your car

Even before you

Have pulled up

Outside my house

I am out of the door

Running barefoot

Down the path

Trying to contain

My excitement

As I wait for you

To alight from the car

Watching as you do

Then throwing myself

Into your arms

Holding you tight

The kiss we share

A kiss of pure love

Of longing

And desire

Too long I have

Been without you

Too long without

Your sweet caress

Looking into

Each other's eyes

Both of us smiling

Unwilling to release

Each other

Then you whisper

The words I've longed to hear

"Hello beautiful, I've missed you".

I Watch.

I watch

As you enter

The room

Smiling

As I see you

Look for me

I watch

You move

Across the room

Smiling

As I see other ladies

Try to catch your eye

I watch

Their faces drop

As you notice me

Smiling

With delight

As your face lights up

I watch

That special twinkle

In your eye

Smiling

As you bend

And kiss my hand

I watch

The look of lust

In your eyes as you stand

Smiling

As you take me

In your arms

I watch

As the room

Seems to disappear

Smiling

As everyone else

Fades into the background

I watch

As your hand

Cups my chin

Smiling

As you tilt my head

Placing a tender kiss on my lips

I watch

As you lead me from the bar

Your possessive arm around my waist

Smiling

At the way

You pull me tight against you

I watch

You open the door

Letting me exit first

Smiling

With love and affection

At the gentleman that has my heart.

Displeased.

I lie here

In the centre

Of my bed

Curled up tight

Trying to make

Myself small

Silent tears

Run across my skin

Eyes swollen

From the hours

Of torturous tears

And thoughts

What have I done?

I don't know

But you've gone

No calls

Or messages

Nothing

Do you love me?

Did you ever?

Or did you say

Those words

To me

To gain my trust?

I love you

I know that much

My heart is shattered

Into a million pieces

As I lie here

In the dark

You have given me

So much joy

Pleasure and confidence

Made me into the

Beautiful woman

You said I was

Gave me the strength

To push myself

To do things

So far out

Of my comfort zone

All to please you

And yet here I am

Alone and crying

For you have gone

Taking the light

Leaving me here

Confidence in tatters

I need you

You are the key

To the lock

Around my heart

The only one

With the power to free me

If only I knew

How and when

I had displeased you

Will you return or is this

The end?

What?

WHAT do you see

When you look at her?

Do you see

Her for who she is

Or who you want her to be?

What do you think

When she enters the room?

Do you think she's beautiful?

Do you see

The confident, sexy woman

Or the scared little girl

That hides inside?

Would you want

To change her?

Or help her

Be the woman

That she could be?

What would you do

To make her strong

And help her feel

Safe and secure?

Would you hold her

Tight when the darkness takes hold?

Would you be the one

To bring the sunshine

And make her blossom?

Would you

Help her grow?

Go on tell her

WHAT you would do.

To Dance.

Candles reflecting

In gilded mirrors

As shadows dance

Around the room

Taking her hand

He leads her

Into the centre

Of the floor

Their song

Begins to play

As they hold

Each other

Slowly

They begin to move

Wrapped in each other

In the moment

Their dance

Of love

Taking them away

To a magical place

Twisting and spinning

As the room around

Them fades

Into the background

Everything

Around them

Forgotten as they

Glide across the floor

Looking deep

Into each other eyes

The love they share

Visible to see

Their hearts beating

In time with each others

As their bodies

Press tightly together

Hearts, minds

And bodies entwined

Souls meeting

And become one

She watches his lips

As he sings

To her

A song filled with love and emotion

Neither of them

Noticing

When the song

Ends

As they continue

To dance

To their own

Private music

The music

Of their union

Music of love

Created by their bodies

In one fluid movement

He sweeps her

Into his arms

Carrying her across the floor

Leaving everyone behind

Escaping to privacy

To continue

Their passionate, sensual dance.

Kiss.

First kiss

Forehead kiss

Kiss filled

With love

Cheek kiss

Get well kiss

Kiss to

Stop the tears

Newborn kiss

Mothers kiss

Kiss to

Say hello

Soft kiss

Hard kiss

Kiss from

A lover

Slow kiss

Intense kiss

Kiss that

Steals your breath

Morning kiss

Loving kiss

Kiss filled

With passion

Wall kiss

Floor kiss

Kiss me

Whenever you want

Lip kiss

Neck kiss

Kiss that

Makes me shudder

Public kiss

Private kiss

Kiss me

Like no other

Lustful kiss

Tender kiss

Kiss to

Show you care

Your kiss

My kiss

Kiss me

Forever.

Perfection.

We walked

Hand in hand

For miles

No words

Passing between us

Just loving glances

And smiles

The beautiful parkland

Empty despite

The heat of the

Summer's day

As you lead me

To my idea

Of heaven

Breath catching

As we enter

The secluded glade

A stream sedately

Running over the

Polished rocks

Of a tiny waterfall

You lead me

To a blanket

That lies beneath

A huge oak

A playful smile

On your lips

As we sit

Soft kisses

Soon becoming

Tempestuous

As passion

Takes over

Tongues engaged

In an erotic dance

The scent of

Summer flowers

Adding to the

Heady, intoxicating

Sensations

That course

Through our bodies

Buttons on

Shirt and dress

Quickly unfastened

Neither of us

Perfect

Yet perfect

For each other

Flaws and issues

Forgotten

Scars unnoticed

As our hands

Gently caress skin

Tracing those scars

And imperfections

Our touch healing

And making perfect

For only the caress

Of a lover

Can make these

Things unimportant

Make them disappear

Our unbridled love

For each other

Healing

Knowing that together

We will help

Each other

Become perfection.

Beautiful?

What is beautiful?

Is it the sunrise

Or sunset?

Is it the flowers

And trees that

Grow all around?

Is it an empty beach

Or beautiful valley?

A mountain

Or a forest?

Nature showing itself

At its best

We forget

These things when

We mention beauty

It seems that

Beauty has become

Something we strive for

Surrounded by images

Of 'perfect' bodies

Of tiny waists

And flat stomachs

Of six packs

And large muscles

Desperate to become

Or have

A glamour model

Or Adonis

Not seeing the beauty

We all possess

But are the models

And the Adonis'

Really that beautiful?

On the outside maybe

But vanity in itself

Is a truly ugly thing

Everybody has

The ability to be beautiful

For true beauty

Comes from the inside

We should all strive to have

Pure hearts and souls

You see everyone

Of us is born beautiful

It's the world around

Us that changes that

Pressure placed on

People to be 'perfect'

If we could change this

Then the world

Could become

A truly wonderful

Beautiful place

Filled with truly

Beautiful people.

There For You.

Why does life

Hurt so much?

Surely this

Isn't normal?

The pain

The anguish

Trying to be

Strong

For friends

That need

Someone strong

To lean on

When they

Never asked

To be in the

Position they are

Being there

To listen

Is the greatest gift

Anyone can give

We all hurt

Some more

Than others

It seems

Feeling every

Ounce of pain

As you have

Pain of your own

But dropping

Everything

To help

A friend

Who needs

You more

Than you know

Until they talk

Flood gates open

All the hurt

And pain pours out

Cleansing

Being able

To share

Lifting the weight

From their shoulders

Watching

As they begin

To shine

The clouds lifting

At times

Like these

We all need

Someone

An ear

A shoulder

To cry on

Or just someone to make you smile

Hurting alone

Isn't healthy

Just know you will

Always have a friend in me.

To Hold.

Stepping from the carriage

The platform full

Of people

All desperate to

Get where they

Are going

Not caring about others

Sinking feeling

As she looks for

Her love

Feeling lost and alone

In a strange city

Wondering which

Way to go

Making her way

Along the platform

Towards the concourse

Pushing her way

Through the throng

Looking at everyone

Hoping to see him

So many faces

Yet none are him

A lump rising

In her throat

As she fights

Through the crowd

And with the tears

Then it happens

Her name called

Through the noise

Turning she sees him

Bags dropped

She runs towards

His strong arms

The tide of people

Seeming to part

Between them

Her tears fall

As they finally

Fall into each

Others arms

Sweeping her

Off her feet

And kissing away

Her tears

They stand there

Wrapped in love

Holding each other tight

The kiss they share

Filled with passion

The platform emptying

As the lovers embrace

Together at last

Love declared

And never to part.

To Be Loved.

How does it feel

To be loved?

The constant sunshine

Big beaming smiles

When you think

Of your love

Your heart racing

And breath catching

Being able to talk

For hours without

Uncomfortable silences

To know that

Just hearing

Each other's voices

Has put a smile

On your faces

That nothing can remove

Finding yourself

Singing along

To happy songs

Without wanting

To cry

A note or message

From your love

Making your heart flutter

Knowing they want you

As much as you want them

Desire and lust coursing

Through your body

At the sound of their voice

Wanting to touch them

To hold them

To spend and eternity

Wrapped in their arms

To walk hand in hand

Proud to be at their side

To stop in the middle

Of the street

Because you need

To hold and kiss

Each other

To want

To need

To love and be loved

Forever and ever

This is what it feels like

To be loved.

Pain.

Sharp

Dull

Intense

Aching

It's

Never

Ending

Heart

Breaking

Tears

Falling

The

Urge

To

Curl

Up

And

Hide

Just

For

A

Moment

To

Escape

How

You

Feel

Inside

To

Ease

The

Pain

Silently

Suffering

Hoping

No

One

Will

Notice

For

Your

Pain

Is

Easier

To

Handle

Than

Theirs

Hurt

And

Pain

Can

Be

Caused

So

Easily

Do

You

Want

To

Continue

With

This

Pain

And

Anguish

Or

Do

You

Run

And

Hide

From

How

You

Truly

Feel?

Demons.

He found her

Curled in a ball

Lying in the

Centre of the bed

She had made herself

Small

Trying to disappear

He recognised the signs

Knew that she

Needed him

Not for passion

But just

To hold her

Whilst she fought

The demons

Inside that

Wanted to do harm

Slipping behind her

Curling his body

Around hers

Wrapping her tight

In his arms

Her tense body

Relaxing

As he whispered

Words of comfort

In her ear

Her sobs fading

As she drew strength

From him

For he is

The light in

The darkness

Her knight in

Shining armour

Again coming to rescue

His damsel in distress

What brought the

Darkness in

This time

He did not know

But he stayed

Holding her

For he loves

And protects her

From all the bad

Both in her head

And out

Their love

Saving her from the demons

That have become weaker

Since he gave

Her his love

And she gave him

Her heart.

Pressure.

The world is full

Of pressure

Pressure to be

Successful

Happy

Rich

In love

Beautiful

To be perfect

Sometimes it would

Be nice to

Have no pressure

To be free to be

Who or what

You want

Not everyone

Can cope with

Pressure

It affects us all

In different

Ways

Some stress

Some strive

Some run

Some hide

For some

How we react

Depends on the situation

Stressing when they have no control

Striving when deadlines loom

Running when it gets too much

Hiding when emotions get involved

How people act

Around us makes

A difference

When under pressure

The last thing you need

Is more pressure

Pressure can build or

Crush a person

Just think

How nice it would be

To live in a world with no pressure.

Love.

That first look

The shy smiles

From that first moment

It was you

Distance no object

For we were

Meant to be

Together

We had a connection

So deep

And strong

It pulled us together

Words not really needed

Our love spoke for us

In conversation

And silence

The spark

That passed between us

As we touched

For the first time

A surge of

Energy

Neither of us

Could deny

That first

Breathtaking kiss

That we never

Wanted to end

The passion and lust

The love and commitment

A bond so strong

That nothing could break it

We are two halves

Of one whole

Our love so strong

And all consuming

It's you

Always was and

Always will be

For you are my one true love.

Anger.

A broken glass

An upturned coffee table

Reminders of the night before

Swollen eyes

Broken hearts

No more tears left to cry

Three simple words

That hurt so deep...

I Hate You

Not meant but still said

Slicing straight

Through your heart

Eyes that blaze

With pain and anger

Hands curled into fists

But left at your side

Turning to leave

Nothing more to say

Is this it?

Is this the end?

The wait to see

What will become

A door finally opened

Breath held

Hands clenched

To stop the shaking

A sick feeling

Deep in the stomach

Then a smile

I'm sorry

Rushing to each other

Arms wrapping tight

As we stand there

Amongst the carnage

Of the tornado

That was our fight

Tears falling

Breathless sobs

Mutual whispers

I love you.

Butterflies.

Sitting here

Gazing out of

The window

Watching beautiful

Butterflies

Flit from flower

To flower

Like snowflakes

In summer

Their colours

So pretty

And bright

As they

Dance and

Flit together

Their dance

So intricate

And complex

As I gaze

I think of you

Wondering

Whether you

Are doing the same

Can you see

The butterflies

Are you thinking of me?

If we were

Together

Would we

Be dancing

The same as

The butterflies

An intricate

Complicated

Dance of love

Or would

Our dance

Be a sensual

One

Us wrapped

And entwined

With each other

Teasingly close

Together

A sexy

Salsa

Or romantic

Rumba

Maybe the passionate

Intensity of an

Argentine tango?

It wouldn't matter

If we were together

I look forward

To the day we

Dance as

The butterflies do

The summer

Sun on our skin

As we move

To our own

Sweet music.

Do You?

Do you

Think of her

When you are alone?

Do you

Wander what

She is doing?

Do you

Feel your heart race

When you think of her?

Do you

Hear her voice

In your dreams?

Do you

Feel her lips

Softly press against yours?

Do you

Smile when you

Hear your song?

Do you

Feel her hand

In yours when you are low?

Do you

Hope that she

Feels yours?

Do you

Wish she was

There with you?

Do you

Hope that one day

Things will be different?

Do you

Cry for what

Could have been?

Do you

Pray for

One more chance?

Do you

Still love her

With all your heart?

Bitch!

Bitch

I gave you everything

Bitch

My heart, my soul, my love

Bitch

Yet it wasn't enough

Bitch

You broke me

Bitch

My world torn to pieces

Bitch

My heart shattered

Bitch

I hope you're happy

Bitch

Yet despite everything

Bitch

I would still give you the world

Bitch

Anything you asked for would be yours

Bitch

I bet you want to know why don't you?

Bitch

Because I **love** you

Angel!

To Be Beautiful.

What would you give

To be beautiful

Forever?

To stay young

Flawless and

Fresh

Would you give anything

Maybe sell your soul to the

Devil?

If all the ugliness and depravity

Could be hidden

Somewhere

Would you pay the price

Become like Dorian

Grey?

Is it a price worth paying

To stay beautiful

Forever?

Or would you prefer

To grow old

Gracefully

And keep your soul

Forever pure and

Free?

Does your beauty live

Only on the

Outside

Or do people see

The beauty that lies

Within?

So again I ask what would

You give to be beautiful

Forever?

Or are you already confident

That your true beauty shines

Through?

A Love Note To You.

As I sit here

At my desk

My thoughts

Turn to you

My love

The CD

Of our songs

Plays

Softly in

The background

The words

Upon the page

Begin to dance

Before my

Tired eyes

As I look

I see the words

Turn into

A love note

For you...

You

I am yours

To please

To tease

To take

And do with

Whatever

You desire

There

Will never

Be anyone

Else for me

My love

For you

Is as constant

As the stars in the sky

Whatever

I'm doing

Wherever

I am

It's

You that

I'm thinking

About

For

You fill

My thoughts

My dreams

Each

Breath I take

Belongs to

You

Every

Smile is

Because I'm

Thinking of you

My

Heart

Body and soul

Are yours

Today

Tomorrow

Eternally

Your good girl.

As sleep steals my sight

Your image appears

In my dreams

And you whisper

I love you too

Tears of happiness

Fall silently

Upon my pillow

And in

My dreams

As your love

Shines through

The darkness

And brings me

Into your light.

Rain.

It doesn't matter

If it's soft

And delicate

Or hard

And punishing

Rain

Hides the tears

That fall

From a

Lost loves

Eyes

Rain

The tears

Mingling

And disappearing

As the drops

Soak skin

Rain

Hides the

Hurt and

Pain like

Nothing

Else can

Rain

Washes away

Grief, anguish

Sorrow and despair

Of a heart that

Is broken

Rain

Every drop

Pushed away

Rolling down

Soft cheeks

Before falling

Rain

Working its

Magic

Hiding the tears

So no one knows

The hurt inside

Rain

After the rain

Has finished

Falling the world

Seems to glow

Under summer sun

Rain

And tears

Replaced by

Heat and light

Heart lifted

And soul brightened

Rain

Without it

Nothing would grow

Without tears

We wouldn't grow

Strong

Rain

Just as the leaves

And flowers

Wouldn't bloom

We wouldn't

Bloom without

Pain

So remember

The pain

Is not forever

It will soon be

Your time to

Bloom.

An Angel Alights.

He stood waiting

The clock striking eight

A time so precise

So there'd be

No mistakes

His suit

Crisp and black

Highlighted

With white

Ready for a night of delights

And then he saw

His angel take

Flight down stairs

Stood before

Shrouded in light

Floating and

Shimmering

Dressed in

Silver

And white

Her smile

Out shining

The stars in the sky

His Venus

Alighting from high

He wanted to take her

Announce to the world

The love that he felt

For his

Gorgeous girl

But their love

Must remain a

Secret untold

For she was a woman

Another did hold

But this night

She was his

To have and to hold

And oh she was

Truly a sight to behold

A kiss oh so

Chaste

Upon soft, sweet flesh

Her breathing did quicken

Shown by her breast

Taking her hand

He led her away

To an evening

Of passion

Not meant to betray

Together they soared

To magical heights

His Lily

Her Evan

Two lovers entwined.

She Sits.

She sits

Silently watching

The rain roll

Down the pane

The storm

So angry

And dark

Yet no match

For the one that

Rages in her heart

Each raindrop

A twin for

Her tears

As she finally

Says goodbye

To her lost love

As much as it hurts

She knows it

Is time

For he is gone

And they will never

Be as one again

Lost and alone

Her heart breaks

But she is strong

She **will** survive

Without him

But he will

Always have a place

In her heart and thoughts

And so

She sits

Letting the tears

Match the rain

Feeling the pain

Drain away

And her strength

Return

The clouds

Finally lifting

Allowing sun

To break

Back into her life

Warming her

For she **is**

A survivor

And she knows

That even though

They were ripped apart

He wouldn't want

Her to sit

At the window

Wasting away

So with his voice

In her head she

Takes a deep breath

And lets the hurt

Slip forever from her life as

She sits.

The Enchantress.

A deep breath

She did take

As she passed

Through the mist

Which shrouded the lake

Solitary trees

Stood guard

Over the tower

Sentries standing

In the barren land

Black as night

Strong and secure

The witch that

Had trapped her love

Was so sure

Sure she wouldn't come

Wouldn't have the strength

To free the man inside

She knew he was waiting

And that gave her strength

Her powers had grown

Stronger since his capture

His love, the enchantress

Would not let

Him down

Dismounting from

Her pure white steed

She felt the witch's presence

Closing her mind

To her hatred

Feeling his love

Pulse through her soul

She walked the last

Few steps to the

Dark tower

She appeared

Her evilness

Shining through

Standing between

The enchantress and love

Their battle was epic

Their powers well matched

Battling with heart and soul

Giving the enchantress

The edge

With a power so strong

She banished the witch

To the land deep below

The devil's mistress

Forever bound

By earth and sulphur

By the devil's own wish

For he had been

Waiting to receive

This fine witch

Weakened by battle

The enchantress did struggle

To the door of the tower

One last chant

And her prince was free

Wrapped in his arms

Her strength did return

She had rescued him

But his love had

Saved her

Together they rode

Through the mist

Towards hopefully

Their happy ever after.

Her Mission.

Bleak open moorland

Was all she could see

The winter wind

So harsh

Whipping

Her heavy woollen cloak

Around her body

She could feel

The fingers of cold

Seeping through

The fabric

Chilling her to her core

Trying to steal

The heat from her heart

Her heart that was

Kept warm by

The love of her prince

And it was for his love

That she was

Walking the moors

In the dead of the night

She had saved him

From entrapment

But it wasn't enough

The spell that was cast

Was stronger than she thought

Her sole mission

For now was to find

The one thing that could save him

Their happy ever after

Had been short lived

Just long enough

For them to declare

Their love for each other

Before he slipped

Into sleep

Unable to wake

So she walked

His only cure

Lay in a cave deep

And dark

She knew there was

A chance she would

Not come out

Alive

But for her prince

She would try

As she approached

The cave

She heard a sound

That chilled her more

Than the wind

A growl, a snarl

A roar

There before her

Was the beast

She did fear

Its eyes locked

On her

Many heads so

Still the beast looked

Like a statue

The feel of

Its putrid breath

Blowing on her face

The only sign it was alive

As she mustered

The strength

To use her powers

To bring the beast

To its knees

Its scaly flesh

Covered

With slime

Made her stomach

Twist

As she fought

To keep the bile

Deep inside

She flinched

As it moved closer

Face to face

They stood

Sizing each other up

Then it reared

And roared

The sound coming from

Each mouth

As it roared

She threw out

Her arms

Drawing more strength

Her every nerve

On fire

As she whispered an

Incantation as old as the land

"Come fire and brimstone

Come rage and anger

Bring heart and passion

And love forever

Take strength

And power from beast

Into my heart

To wake and save

The prince of my heart"

Her hands reaching forward

The force from within

Her soul

Flying out through

Her fingertips

The magic so strong

That the light was blinding

Then she felt it

The power

From the beast

Filling her body

Without a glance

She turned and fled

Turning her back

On the place filled with dread

Each step was a struggle

For although she had won

The battle continued

To rage in her soul

As the beast tried to win

From deep within

Her strength failing

As she returned to

Her prince

She cried when she saw

The castle loom large

Her journey near

Over as she flew to his side

Her lips upon his

One final kiss

She did give to him

Her gift was the power

From the beast within

The spell it did break

But also her heart

Her mission was over

The prince she did save

But her life force

Was drained

She had given her all

To save her true love

From deaths door

He wept as he held her

As she slipped from

This world

Pulling her closer

To hear her last words

As she drew her

Final breath

She whispered

I love you my prince

Before fading away.

Thank You's.

To my family, as always without your backing, support and love none of my work would ever come to pass. You never fail to amaze me with your strength and love and I am truly grateful and love you all with all my heart.

To Dympna, Paula and Steve, thank you for being there for me, for pushing me and for putting up with my doubts and questions. Your support means the world to me.

And finally to everyone else that has supported me in my crazy ambition to get my words out there for people to read, you guys rock.

Much love,

S.J xx

Made in the USA
Charleston, SC
24 May 2015